T0197385

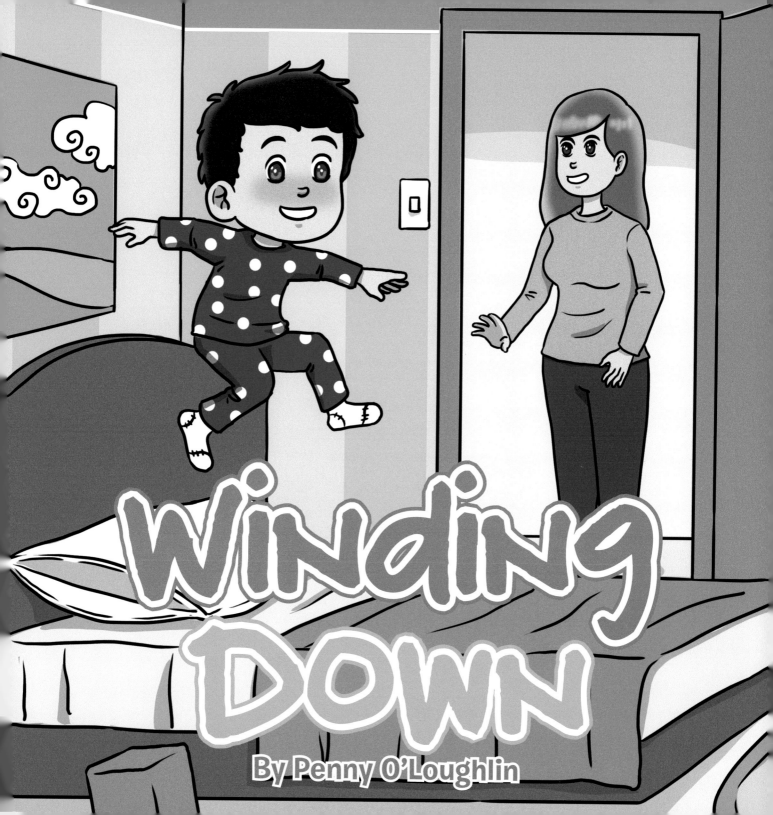

# Winding Down

By Penny O'Loughlin

To order additional copies of this book, contact:
Xlibris
AU TFN: 1 800 844 927 (Toll Free inside Australia)
AU Local: 0283 108 187 (+61 2 8310 8187 from outside Australia)
www.xlibris.com.au
Orders@Xlibris.com.au

ISBN:   Softcover        978-1-6641-0357-3
        Hardcover        978-1-6641-0358-0
        EBook            978-1-6641-0359-7

Print information available on the last page

Rev. date: 03/31/2021

Dedicated to my
firecracker, Fletcher.

Blanket up,
Snuggle in tight.
It's time for bed–
Time to turn out the light.

The pillow is soft,
So relax your head.
The blanket is warm
In your cosy bed.

Let all your thoughts
Just pass by,
Like fluffy white clouds
Sweeping the sky.

Close your eyes now,
'Til it be dawn.
The moon is out,
The curtains drawn.

Slow down your legs,
Relax your body all through,
Wind down your heartbeat,
And relax your mind too.

Deep breaths out,
Count one ... two ... and three.
The day's noise has gone,
It's just you and me.

Smile at the memories
Of your wonderful day.
Let them warm your heart
As you hear Mummy say:

"Goodnight, my darling.
We love you so.
Be free from all worries;
Just let them go."

"Feel safe and secure
All the night through
As you bask in our love
And feel it surround you."

"Let go of the day.
Snuggle in tight.
Sweet dreams, magnificent boy.
Escape peacefully.
Goodnight."

Printed in the United States
by Baker & Taylor Publisher Services